DINO KNIGHTS
EXTINCTION

DINO KNIGHTS
EXTINCTION

JEFF NORTON
ILLUSTRATED BY JEFF CROSBY

Scallywag Press Ltd
LONDON

First published in 2025 by Scallywag Press Ltd.,
10 Sutherland Row, London SW1V 4JT

Text © Jeff Norton, 2025
Illustrations © Jeff Crosby, 2025

The rights of Jeff Norton and Jeff Crosby to be identified
as the author and illustrator of this work have been asserted by them
in accordance with the Copyright, Designs and Patents Act, 1988
All rights reserved.

Printed and bound in China on FSC paper
by C&C Offset Printing Co. Ltd

001

British Library Cataloguing in Publication Data available

ISBN 978-1-83630-008-3

*For Sidonie…
for always believing.*

J.N.

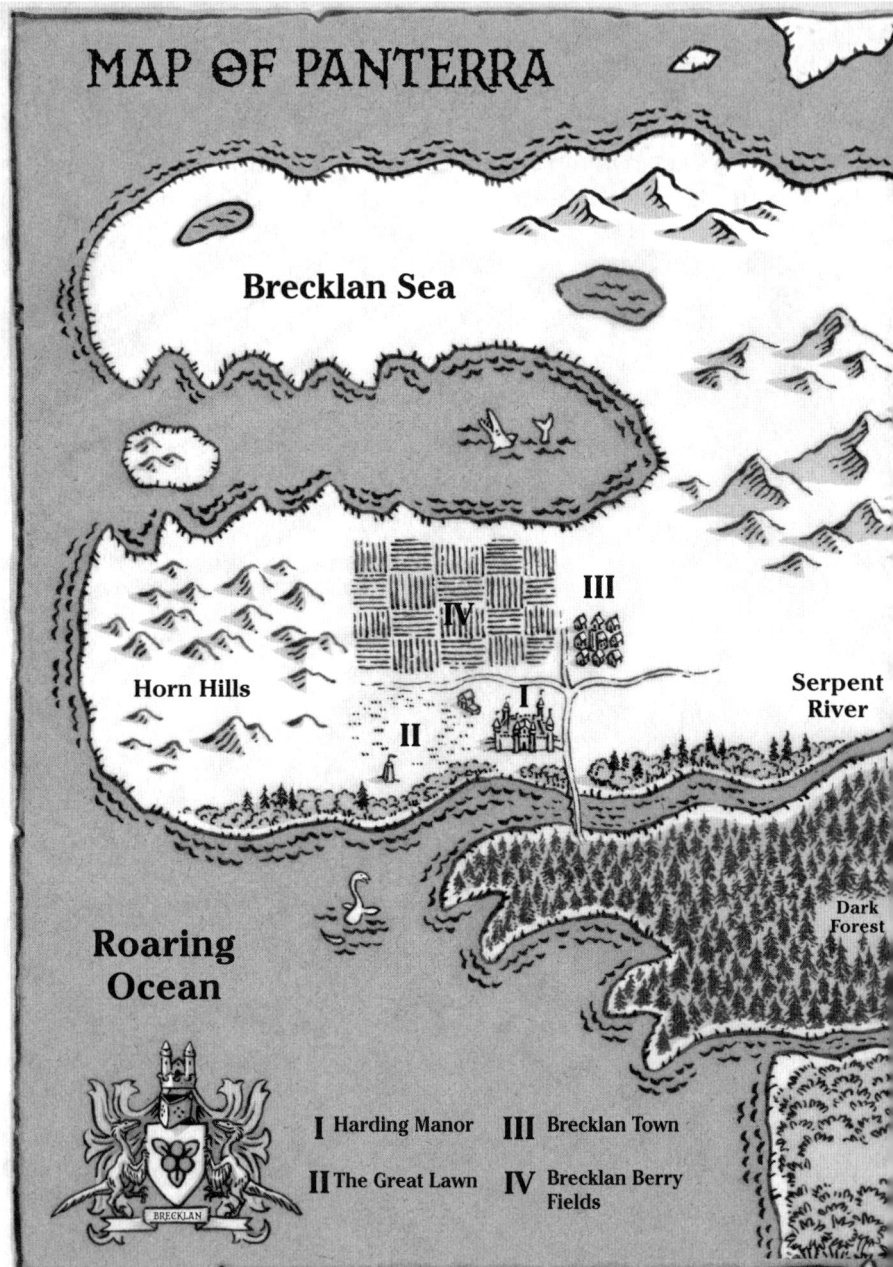

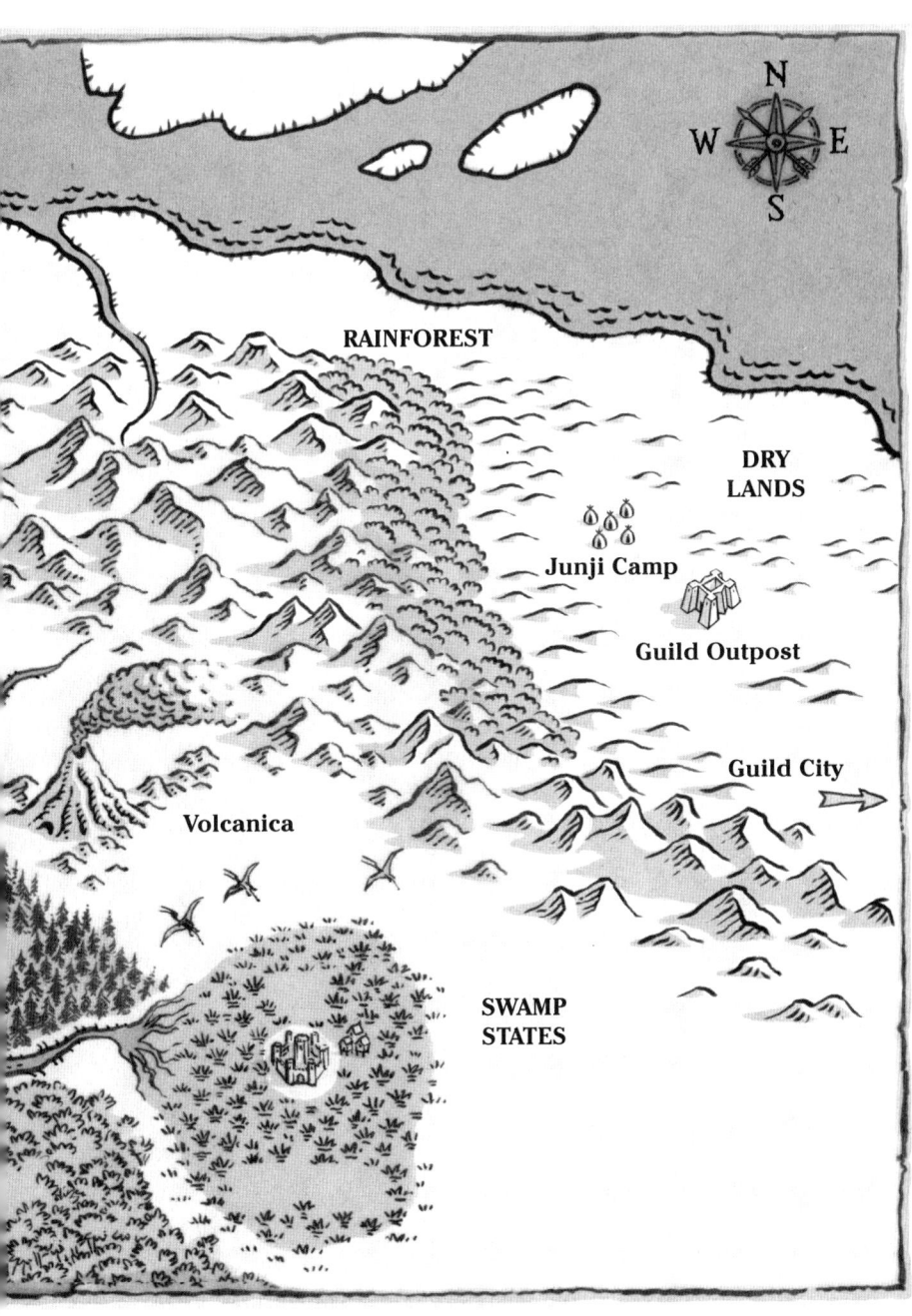

Lord Harding
Longtime ruler of Brecklan, and Henry's guardian.

Lady Anwyn
Wise co-ruler of Brecklan, and champion of peace.

Captain Carey
Commander of the Guild's western outpost.

General Razzath
Ruthless Guild general, determined to kill all dinosaurs.

Hannah
Warrior of the Junji, ancient tribe of the Dry Lands.

Hera
Hannah's mother, tribal elder of the Junji.

Sylvia and Harris
Henry's parents, missing since he was a baby.

Cylis
Warrior of the Swamp States

Henry Fairchild loved riding his dinosaur into battle.

He raised his sword, ready to strike as he raced towards his opponent on the back of his trusty Tyrannosaur, Rex. Henry was a Dino Knight, a trained warrior and defender of Brecklan, his beloved homeland.

The young knight's armour had been polished to a shine, reflecting the bright sun above. He trained his gaze on the leather-clad figure riding towards him on a pterosaur, its wings tucked in for the charge. The two fighters held their swords high. Only one would prevail.

Henry gripped the reins with his left hand as he ducked his helmeted head, swiping his blade at his fast-approaching opponent.

THUMP!

The young soldier fell from his winged steed as a deafening cheer erupted from the home-town crowd. Henry had been so focused that he'd almost forgotten this was not a real battle, but a simulated one – a game, and a friendly one at that.

Their contest was part of the first-ever Friendship Games that Brecklan was hosting with its neighbours, many of whom had been at war with Henry's homeland not so long ago. The games were part of Lord Harding's plan to bring lasting peace to the realm of Panterra.

"Better to clash metal in tournament than on the field of battle," he had explained to the Dino Knights, when he proposed his plan for the games.

Henry leapt down from Rex and faced his opponent on the field. All around him, the spectators in the wooden stands cheered him on.

But Henry's opponent was not yet ready to concede.

The fighter smirked at Henry as he clutched his sword in two hands, eager to defend himself at ground level.

"Ready to yield?" asked Henry.

"You wish, Breck," came the reply.

"My name is Henry, actually."

"Well, Henry Actually, I'm Cylis, but my opponents know me as Victor."

Henry had to admire the boy's confidence. They were roughly the same age, but while Cylis was taller and looked stronger, Henry was both fast and clever. "Then let's give them a show, Cylis Victor," he replied.

Henry swung his sword, which Cylis met in mid-air with his own.

CLANK!

Sparks flew as metal struck metal.

The fighters clashed dramatically, giving the audience more of a theatrical performance than a real fight.

At one point, Henry swung at Cylis's head, but Cylis did a backflip to avoid the blade and turned to bow to the crowd.

Henry let him have his moment before going on the attack again.

"Is that all you've got?" goaded Cylis.

Henry aimed for his legs, but Cylis blocked the blow.

THWACK!

"I'm just getting started," Henry replied with a smile. "Rex!"

Henry's dinosaur charged forwards and twisted around, offering his tail to his master. Henry hopped onto it and Rex lifted it up. Henry rose above Cylis and took advantage of his new-found height to leap down on Cylis, forcing him to the ground. Henry held his sword flat against his opponent.

"Now will you yield?" Henry asked.

"Fine," relented Cylis. "You win, Breck."

Henry stood up and offered his hand to Cylis. The crowd clapped, both at the spectacle and the sportsmanship.

Henry waved to the crowd, soaking up the applause. He then turned to Cylis. "It's too bad you're a Swamp Rat and not a Breck. We could use someone like you fighting alongside the Dino Knights."

"Maybe, but us Swamp Rats fly graceful pterosaurs, not plodding dinosaurs. And if my Hetty had been allowed to use her wings in this bout, I could have used height to my advantage. I prefer to fly than ride."

Henry nodded and smiled. He had flown on the back of a pterosaur once and it was exhilarating. That was back when the Swamp States was an enemy of Brecklan. But now the only battles between neighbours took place here on the tournament grounds. Henry realised that Lord Harding was right, as usual –

it was far better to fight in friendly competition than in fierce battle.

Cylis nodded at two older spectators in the front row of the stands. They responded with a friendly wave.

"Your fans?" asked Henry.

"My parents," Cylis replied. "They didn't want to miss my debut tournament, but I just hope I didn't disappoint them by losing."

"You didn't lose, Cylis," Henry reassured him. "You fought hard and represented the Swamp States with honour."

Henry turned to Cylis's parents and tilted his head towards their son, silently acknowledging that he had been a worthy competitor.

But in that instant, with hundreds of spectators watching him, Henry Fairchild felt very much alone. He reminded himself that he belonged to a team, the Dino Knights, and he lived in the close-knit community of Brecklan Town, but unlike Cylis, he had never known his parents, and probably never would. It was a great hole in his heart. And that absence, that terrible sense of not knowing what happened to them, gnawed at his soul.

His parents had ventured east and never returned. But why?

Henry looked east towards the great mountains that rose up into the clouds, with no idea of what lay beyond them. He vowed to himself he would do whatever it took to discover what had befallen his missing parents.

"You want to do *what*?" gasped Gally.

Henry leant against Rex as the flames of the campfire kept the Dino Knights warm on the cool, clear night. The other dinosaurs were resting in their pens, but Rex never went to sleep before Henry, always staying by his master's side. High above them, the chalk-white moon glowed brilliantly in the star-filled sky; a perfect circle except for a missing fragment, as if a giant had taken a bite out of a biscuit.

"You heard me," Henry replied. He had just told his friends about his plan to travel east.

"But we are needed here," asserted Torin, leader of the group. "Brecklan may be at peace, but it's our job to keep it that way. And we can only do that by riding high, on our dinos, *here*, in our homeland."

Henry knew Torin was making a pointed comment about him. Less than a year ago, Henry had defied Lord Harding's orders and left Brecklan with Ellie, one of the other Dino Knights, to save her people in the Highlands. While they were gone, the conniving Prince Pattick had invaded Brecklan. The incursion was daring and ruthless, but the Dino Knights eventually regrouped and repelled the attack, restoring peace to their corner of Panterra. Since then, Lord Harding and the Dino Knights had brokered peace deals with all of Brecklan's neighbours. But Torin liked to remind the team that they needed to stick together, and that peace was precarious.

Ellie leapt to Henry's defence. "When my family was in trouble, Henry didn't hesitate to help," she said.

"That's because he's reckless," said Gally, spoiling for an argument.

"That's not fair," said Iyla, the scientist of the group. "Henry and Ellie did what was right, even if it wasn't what was allowed. And now, if Henry wants to go east and find out what happened to his parents, I vote we have his back."

"Aye," agreed Ellie in her Highland accent, raising her hand to be counted.

"Nobody's voting," said Gally.

Torin frowned, as he considered his options. This was a difficult decision. "We would need Harding's blessing, Henry," he said.

"And you shall have it," came a voice from the darkness.

Lord Harding stepped into the orange firelight and leant on his walking stick, which was fashioned from dinosaur bone. Lady Anwyn, fellow benefactor of the Dino Knights, stood by his side. The team rose to greet them.

"At ease, knights," Lord Harding said. "We were just out for an evening stroll when we overheard your discussion. The last thing we want is for any of you to go galloping off in the middle of the night.

No, we would much rather know what you're up to and deal with it in the light of day – or should I say, the light of this fire."

"But we're not galloping anywhere," Gally protested. "We've got no idea what lies beyond the mountains."

"Perhaps it's time to venture into the unknown, Galliard," replied Lady Anwyn. "Not only to find out what happened to Henry's parents, but also to discover what is on the other side of the mountain range, be it friend or foe. We have seen what happens when we don't understand our neighbours, and when we don't talk to them. Suspicion leads to fear, and fear leads to war. If we want to pursue our great cause of peace in Panterra, we need to know who we are trying to make peace with."

Henry could see that even Gally was following her logic.

Lord Harding carried on where Lady Anwyn had left off. "You Dino Knights are not just warriors," he said. "You're also ambassadors. You represent the very best of Brecklan, and we trust you to trek across the mountain range and explore the lands beyond."

"Are those your orders?" asked Torin.

"No," replied Lord Harding. "Not orders, but wishes. We won't command you to undertake this venture – you must *choose* to do so. As a team."

"And, Henry," Lady Anwyn added, placing her hand on his shoulder, "we both hope you find what you're looking for."

"Thank you, my lady," Henry replied, grateful for her kindness and support.

"And I hope you know what you're doing," Gally muttered under his breath.

Ellie heard this and punched his arm.

"Then we ride," announced Torin. "For Brecklan."

"For Brecklan!" the other four cheered in unison, Gally somewhat reluctantly.

The next few days were a flurry of activity for the Dino Knights.

Iyla took charge of the equipment, carefully packing the dinosaurs' cargo bags and arming the expedition. Henry and Ellie visited her laboratory to offer their help, and from the range of weapons piled on her workbench, it seemed as if Iyla meant to take the entire armoury.

"You can never be too careful," Iyla declared. "Or too heavily armed."

"Ha!" Henry laughed. "Just remember our dinos have to carry everything over the mountain range."

"And I don't want my Kayla to carry anything explosive," warned Ellie. "Things that go boom make her very nervous."

Me too, thought Henry.

"Iyla, let me help you get this stack of weapons down to a more manageable stockpile," he offered.

Meanwhile, Gally kept to the kitchen of Harding Manor with the head cook, planning meals for the trek. "An army marches on its stomach," he had declared. "And I like my marching to be fuelled by the finest ingredients."

Ellie had gone to join Torin in the library, where Henry later found them both studying maps of the great mountain range.

"I think we've found the quickest pass across the peaks," Ellie shared. "But that's as far as the maps go."

"I wonder what we'll find on the other side?" mused Torin.

Henry consulted some books for clues on what might lie ahead on their journey, but could not find any reliable accounts of Panterra to the east. There were rumours, like the idea that Panterra ended on a great cliff edge into nothingness. He even read somewhere that the east was filled with flying dinosaurs called 'dragons' that shot fire from their snouts. As he scoured the library shelves, Henry found several volumes that might provide a nugget of truth beyond the myths. One was particularly compelling – it was a folk tale called Spirits of the East, and told the chilling tale of Renseith, an intrepid Breck who travelled east to seek his fortune, only to find a dense rainforest haunted by the ghosts of long-dead dinosaurs.

It was a frightening read, making Henry doubt whether venturing into the vast unknown was a good idea after all. But he was determined in his quest and encouraged by his friends' willingness to help.

On their last night in Brecklan, the Dino Knights gathered around their nightly campfire. It had become a tradition to swap stories around the fire, so Henry decided to tell the ghost story he had read earlier.

"I'm not afraid of ghosts," Gally scoffed. "Running out of pudding is what scares me!"

Torin rolled his eyes. "I did hear from Cook that you've swiped all his desserts."

They all laughed. It was typical of Gally to put his needs first, but secretly each of the Dino Knights was pleased that there would be a sweet taste of home on their expedition.

Ellie spoke next, sharing her ghost story.

It was a tale about a spectre that had haunted the Highlands for years. Finally, one night, her uncle Angus confronted the ghost and learnt it simply wanted to rest each night in its former home. From then on, Angus left the door unlatched at night and the ghost let itself in, curled up by the fire and didn't bother anyone ever again.

This time it was Iyla who huffed. "That's not very scary, Ellie!" she said.

"I guess the point of my tale," her friend replied briskly, "is ye've got to confront your fear, otherwise it haunts you forever."

Henry thought about that. The fate of his parents was something he'd always wondered about and had never had courage to face. But in his quiet moments, and in his dreams, it did haunt him.

Ellie was right. It was time to confront his fear.

Morning came early for Henry. The sun edged over the eastern mountain range as Henry saddled Rex up with Iyla's cargo bags of supplies and weapons. The Dino Knights assembled on the grounds of Harding Manor, the campfire still smouldering in the morning dew.

Sunlight crept across the great lawn,

illuminating the five young knights and their devoted dinosaurs.

Torin rode his loyal Nothronychus Haringey – or Harry, as Henry had nicknamed him. Harry was alert, with fine feathers and a quick wit. Iyla climbed atop Conker, her hefty Anklyosaur. Conker was covered in thick scales, and his tail ended with a rock-like club that could topple a castle turret with a single swing. Henry didn't dare give him a nickname.

Ellie's Kayla was a gentle Styracosaurus with six imposing spikes. Gally's dino, Avin, was an Ornithomimus, the smallest of the group's dinos, but also the fastest. Henry was sure Avin longed to be a pterosaur – he loved leaping so much, riding him felt like flying. Just like his master, Avin liked to show off and enjoyed being the centre of attention.

Finally, Henry climbed aboard his Tyrannosaurus, whom he had named Rex at their first meeting, when the wild dino had threatened Lord Harding and Lady Anwyn's carriage. Boy and dino had come a long way together since that fateful day, when Henry demonstrated that he had a special connection to dinosaurs and an uncanny ability to commune with them. Indeed, Henry felt a deep love for the dino he had adopted that day. Rex wasn't a pet, he was a partner, and Henry was convinced Rex felt the same way about him.

Lord Harding and Lady Anwyn emerged from the great manor house. They greeted the Dino Knights.

"And so it begins," Lord Harding declared.

Lady Anwyn looked at Henry with kind eyes and smiled. "Henry, I know you seek answers about your parents, but always remember you have a home in Brecklan, and no matter what happens beyond those mountains, you have a family here."

Henry nodded, returning the smile.

"Dino Knights," said Lord Harding. "There is no challenge you cannot overcome if you work together as a team. Now go, discover what lies beyond the mountains, and Henry, I sincerely hope your quest is a success."

"Thank you," Henry said.

With that, Torin took up the reins of Haringey and led the Dino Knights down the long road out of the grounds. Henry glanced up at the mountains, the sun now clearing the peak, and breathed in with both excitement and trepidation.

"No going back now," he whispered to Rex.

The Dino Knights reached the foothills quickly and began climbing. To the north, the path that led to the Highlands was well travelled, but going east, the group had to forge their own way up the steep slope.

After a while they found a dry stream bed to use as a way up towards the peaks. In the springtime, snow melt would channel this way down the mountain, but now, in late summer, the stream had gone, providing a useful route to follow.

At Gally's urging, the expedition stopped for lunch around midday. Henry wanted to keep going, but he couldn't ignore the rumblings of his own stomach. They'd had breakfast before dawn, and both the knights and their dinos welcomed a rest from the punishing climb.

Henry gazed down on Brecklan and out to the vast sea beyond. He noticed the sea simply stopped at the horizon, and for a moment he wondered if the myths were true: did the world really end at the edge of a cliff?

But Henry didn't want to believe that. He wanted to believe there was something beyond the horizon, just as he needed to believe there was something, and hopefully someone, waiting for him on the other side of the mountain range.

After a short break, the group resumed their trek – Torin wanted to reach the other side of the mountains before nightfall. As they approached the summit, the sun began to sink in the west, mirrored in the ocean. Henry took one last look back at the world he knew. The group then entered a narrow pass between two craggy peaks. As they emerged on the other side, the weather was decidedly different.

A thick fog enveloped them as they made their way down the far side of the mountains. As darkness fell, it became too dangerous to continue, and Torin ordered the team to stop for the night. Ellie and Gally pitched tents, whilst Iyla used her fire-starter to make a campfire from some sage brush that Henry and Torin had gathered. The fire kept them warm as they ate, but nobody felt like telling ghost stories in the fog. They were all exhausted, so sleep came easily.

In the morning, the group ate their breakfast rolls – eggs and cheese in a soft bun – and packed up quickly, setting off through lingering mist. Soon they reached the tree line of a mountain rainforest. Henry remembered the tale of Reinseth, hoping they would not encounter any ghosts or spirits as they ventured through the increasingly dense vegetation.

The dinos were happy, because large, berry-like fruits weighed down many of the rainforest trees. The plant-eaters among them snacked as they walked, but Rex, a true carnivore, left the fruit alone. Henry fretted about this, aware that at some point his dinosaur would need to feast to stay strong.

After a few hours of slow descent, the trees thinned out and the air became warmer and drier. Henry and Rex emerged into bright sunlight, stopping to take in a strange landscape. The barren plain spreading out below them was yellowish-brown with a tint of orange –
an endless sea of sand leading to the horizon, and interrupted only by the odd herd of roaming dinosaurs.

"Great," huffed Gally. "It's a big empty space."

"Look more closely," urged Iyla, pointing to what appeared to be a cluster of triangles in the distance.

"Could be a settlement," Torin mused.

"Signs of life," said Ellie. "Let's go see."

They made their way down the mountains' sandy foothills, getting closer to what looked like an encampment of maybe a hundred tents. But then Henry spotted something else.

At least ten triangles had left the camp and were heading towards them at high speed. At first, Henry thought they were some kind of flying tent, but as they approached, he realised the moving triangles were in fact sails, and part of boat-like contraptions, attached to wheels.

"Something tells me this isn't a welcome party," said Iyla as they reached the flat desert.

"Let's not jump to conclusions," urged Torin. "But keep your weapons to hand."

"Uncle Angus always used to tell me to tread softly and carry a big axe," said Ellie.

"He's a wise man," Torin replied grimly.

The land-boats were almost upon them. They harnessed the wind that swept across the desert, racing across the flat land faster than a sprinting velociraptor.

"I'm glad I'm riding a T-Rex," muttered Henry, gripping Rex's reins.

"We should strike first," urged Gally, fear creeping into his voice. "Show them we mean business."

"But we don't even know who they are!" protested Iyla.

Torin called for calm. "Remember, Lord Harding wants diplomacy, not war. Let's hear them out but hold our ground."

Henry counted twelve land-boats in all. He could now see they were as big as the canoes they'd used to launch the attack against Pattick, when the tyrant's forces invaded Brecklan. The sails were branded with a black dinosaur skull on top of two crossed bones. Henry wasn't sure what that meant, but it didn't seem friendly.

Each craft had a crew of dark-haired warriors wearing dino hides. As the land-boats slowed, they encircled the Brecks and lowered their sails, training their harpoons on the dinosaurs.

Torin lifted his hand in greeting. "We are explorers in your land and have travelled from far away. We come in peace."

"And yet you ride beasts and carry weapons of war," replied one of the captains, seemingly the leader of the fleet. She had long black hair and deep

dark eyes that showed no emotion. Henry guessed she was about his age, maybe a bit older.

Iyla stepped forward and raised her hand. "The weapons were my idea," she admitted. "You can never be too prepared."

Ellie kept her sword sheathed but did not take her eyes off the harpoon launchers. "Sail softly and carry sharp harpoons," she murmured under her breath. These desert-faring warriors clearly thought like her uncle.

Henry decided to try his hand at diplomacy. "We are the Dino Knights of Brecklan, and my name is Henry Fairchild," he said. "Our weapons are only for our own defence."

Their young leader spoke again. "I am Hannah of the Junji, ancient tribe of the Dry Lands," she stated. "And your incursion into our land is an act of war."

"I told you we should have attacked first," whispered Gally.

"We do not seek war," Henry replied, ignoring Gally's comment.

Hannah looked straight at Henry with cold eyes. "Begone, Dino Knights of Brecklan, or prepare to die!" she said.

Henry gulped. He didn't exactly like either option.

IV

Henry tried not to look at the harpoons aimed squarely at the five dinosaurs.

"Hannah of the Junji," he said softly. "We need your help."

This seemed to confuse her. She glanced at the other boat captains, checking their reactions. They seemed equally wrong-footed by Henry's show of vulnerability.

"Henry speaks the truth," added Torin. "We seek assistance, not conflict."

"Then state your case," Hannah demanded.

Torin motioned to Henry to continue.

"We are on a quest to find out what happened to my parents, who were lost long ago. They came over the mountains when I was just a baby and were never heard of again."

Hannah stood silent for what felt like forever. Something in her expression softened.

"Not to know your family is a curse. It's as if your history has been stolen from you," she said at last. "The Junji can trace our bloodlines back to the first tribes that sailed these deserts, and long before that, to when all of this was water and not sand."

"I just want to know what happened to my parents," Henry pleaded quietly.

"That is a worthy quest," the desert warrior agreed. "But nonetheless, you have invaded our lands, so you must suffer the consequences."

"Begone or prepare to die ..." repeated Henry. "Maybe there's a third option?"

"Maybe," pondered Hannah. "We shall take you prisoner and present you to our tribal elder. She can determine your fate."

"And help with my quest?" Henry asked.

"That is not up to me," Hannah replied. "But our tribal elder is wise, and not unkind."

Gally offered up his wrists to be tied together. "Okay then, take us to your leader," he said.

Iyla scoffed at him. "First you want to fight, and now you want to surrender."

"No, Iyla, Gally is right," Torin interjected. "We will go willingly with Hannah to seek an audience with her tribe's elder."

"Perhaps we could travel as your guests, Hannah," suggested Henry, "and not as your prisoners."

"Perhaps," she agreed, eyeing Rex with wonder. "On one condition."

"Go on," Henry said with a smile. He had a good idea what Hannah was about to ask.

"You ride these wild beasts as if they are your ... pets. Could I ride one too?"

Henry patted Rex on the neck. "What do you think, Rex? Room for another?"

Rex snorted, which Henry took as a yes.

"You heard him," said Henry. "Climb aboard!"

Hannah jumped off her land-boat and approached the mighty T-Rex. Rex lowered himself and Henry offered

Hannah his hand, to pull her up onto his dino's back. She sat behind Henry's saddle and laughed out loud.

"Look at me," she called to her people. "I'm riding a beast!"

The rest of the Junji looked on in amazement. It suddenly occurred to Henry that without the Brecklan Berries they used back home to tame the dinosaurs, the dinos here in the Dry Lands would be wild and dangerous. It was no wonder Hannah was so excited by the prospect of riding a dinosaur. Even for Henry, it was still an incredible thrill.

"We call them dinosaurs," Henry said. "And to us, they are more than animals. They are a part of our team. They're not pets – they're partners."

"Then let's ride!" Hannah called. "Partner!"

The Junji raised their sails and accompanied the five dinosaurs towards the camp. Henry held on to Rex's reins and Hannah held on to Henry. Rex carried them at a quick and rhythmic pace.

"Enjoying the ride?" Henry asked his passenger.

"It's incredible!" Hannah exclaimed, her hair whipping in the wind. "We live alongside beasts – I mean, dinosaurs – but I never imagined I would ever get to ride one."

In the distance, Henry spotted a wild Stenonychosaurus herd racing over the desert sands. Like a flock of birds, the group changed direction upon hearing the convoy. Henry marvelled at how they operated almost as one body.

"Do they roam freely here?" asked Henry, keen to learn more about the Dry Lands.

"Most of them live in herds, but some live alone," she explained. "For us, the dinosaurs provide much of what we need. We use their bones to build land-boats and our shelters. We use their hides as clothing and to cover our tents. And we eat their meat to stay alive."

Rex growled and Henry gasped. The idea of eating dinosaur disgusted Henry, and he stroked Rex to reassure him he didn't see him as a meal.

"Sorry, Rex," Hannah said, stroking his neck. "It's just the way of the desert. But we never take more than we need. We try to live in harmony with dinosaurs, and with the land. But others here have different ideas."

Hannah pointed to some dark shapes in the distance. As they got closer, Henry could smell the rotting flesh before he could see the carnage. It was a pack of eight dead Parasaurolophuses, lying motionless in the sand under the hot sun. Rex reared up in horror, almost bucking off his riders.

"Don't come close!" Henry called back to the Dino Knights, who were following behind.

"What happened?" shouted Ellie, covering her nose.

"The Guild slaughtered these creatures for sport," Hannah said, shaking her head with sadness and disgust.

"What's the Guild?" Henry asked.

"An enemy of these lands," she replied. "And something to be feared."

As the group approached the Junji encampment, Hannah issued a warning. "Let me do the talking," she said. "My people are suspicious of strangers."

When the Dino Knights and land-boats stopped at the camp perimeter, Henry saw what Hannah had meant about using the dinosaurs for everything they needed.

The tents were pitched over tall bones and covered with stretched dino hide. He was impressed by the tribe's ingenious use of natural resources in their harsh environment. At least the Junji didn't kill dinosaurs for sport, like the mysterious Guild did. Henry was eager to learn more about the Guild, but first he and the other Dino Knights had to be introduced to the Junji elder.

Henry and Hannah dismounted first.

"Hannah, my child, you have returned with beast-riding strangers," called a woman with greying hair, sitting on a large chair of hide and bone. Henry figured she was the one in charge.

"They are on a noble quest, Mother," replied Hannah. "These are the Dino Knights, who come from a faraway land called Brecklan, over the western mountains."

So Hannah is the elder's daughter, thought Henry. *She kept that quiet.*

The rest of the Junji, nearly a hundred strong, had assembled to gawk at the newcomers astride their tame beasts. Henry heard murmurs of suspicion and confusion.

"Nonsense!" the elder scolded Hannah. "Nothing exists beyond the mountains."

Torin gave a small cough. "We do, um, your Elderness," he said. "I am Torin, leader of the Dino Knights. We offer you the hand of friendship."

"And I am Hera," she replied. "I also lead. It seems we have that in common."

"Perhaps we have much in common," suggested Torin, climbing down off Haringey and bowing respectfully to Hera. "May I present to you my fellow Dino Knights – Galliard, Elspeth, Iyla and Henry."

Following Torin's lead, they climbed

down from their dinos to bow deeply to the tribal elder.

"At least you strangers have manners," Hera said. "Maybe you could teach my daughter some."

"Mother!" snapped Hannah. "This is hardly the time or—"

"Like when I say it's time to study ancient texts," interrupted Hera, "and she takes off into the desert without my permission."

"We are not so different, ma'am," persisted Torin. "For only recently, Ellie and Henry set off without our master's permission, which led to a whole heap of trouble."

Ellie cleared her throat to protest, but it was Henry who spoke first. "With respect, Torin, this is hardly the time or the place."

Hera laughed. "Much in common, indeed! I suppose it is the nature of the young to defy the old. Now, Hannah, tell me about this quest."

Hannah repeated what Henry had told her, and her mother listened carefully.

"Over time, there has been talk of strangers from afar," she said, turning to Henry. "But I do not know your parents, young man."

"Could they have encountered the Guild?" he asked. Perhaps this would give him some clue as to his family's whereabouts.

"For their sakes, I hope not," replied Hera. "The Guild hail from the east, from cities that are diseased and overcrowded. They come here to clear the desert of beasts and build settlements. These people are cruel and do not live in harmony with the land." She pointed towards the vast landscape beyond the encampment. "They know nothing of our ways and believe all this belongs to them."

Henry could now understand why the Junji were so suspicious of strangers.

"And just two nights ago the Guild ransacked our camp," Hera continued. "They stole our aqua jewels."

"What are aqua jewels?" asked Henry, glancing at Hannah.

"They are special jewels, of different minerals and colours," Hannah explained. "The tribes of the Dry Lands use aqua jewels to barter for water rights. Without a good supply to trade with, we Junji will die of thirst."

Hera got up from her chair. "Water is the lifeblood of all things in the Dry Lands," she said. "And so we must be wary of the hot sun. Now, Hannah, help your friends get settled in and move their beasts into the shade. Give them all something to eat and drink."

With that, Hera signalled that the meeting was over. There was a lot to do; while the Dino Knights set up a temporary pen for their dinosaurs, Hannah gathered a group of workers to construct shelters to protect them from the blazing heat. Brecklan's temperate climate meant the dinos were not used to such extreme conditions.

And neither were the Knights, who were sweltering in their armour.

"Let's find you all something cooler to wear," said Hannah, offering them a welcome change of clothes. The Dino Knights' new soft dino hide tunics were lighter and much better suited to the desert.

Hannah helped Henry adjust his tunic. "You've got it on backwards, silly," she laughed.

"I've never worn a dino hide before," he protested, still not sold on the idea, however practical it might be.

"There you go," said Hannah, turning the tunic round so Henry could push his arms through. "Much better. You look like a Junji now."

"Thanks," said Henry. "So, Hannah, your mother is the leader of your tribe? You didn't mention that before."

"Yes," said Hannah, with a sigh. "And in time I will take over as elder. It is the way of the Junji, but ..."

She trailed off.

"But what?" asked Henry.

"I'm not sure I want the responsibility. To lead my people will be a great burden."

"Yes," agreed Henry. "But it's also a privilege. And you seem like a natural leader."

Hannah thought about that and laughed. To his surprise, Henry liked the fact that he could make her smile.

"Are you two finished playing dress up?" asked Ellie, striding over in her Junji outfit.

Henry thought she seemed annoyed, but couldn't understand why.

"He fits right in," said Hannah.

"Sure," said Ellie, with a hint of snark in her voice.

That evening, as the sun dipped below the mountain, the Junji set up fires to keep themselves warm. It made Henry a touch homesick for the Dino Knight campfires back on the lawn of Harding Manor.

Torin called a meeting for the Dino Knights. He had spent the rest of the afternoon talking with Hera and had some important things to tell the group. "Hera has asked for our help," he said. "She wants us to go after the Guild, to get the Junji's precious aqua jewels back. I told her, respectfully, that this was not our mission. We can't go picking fights with forces we know nothing about."

Henry was shocked. "But, Torin, you heard what Hannah said," he cried. "Without those jewels, the Junji won't be able to trade for water. It's literally their lifeline. We have to help."

Ellie scoffed. "Henry just wants to impress his girlfriend," she said.

"Look who's jealous of her boyfriend!" Gally smirked, making Ellie scowl.

"Enough!" called Torin. "I'm the leader of this group, and I'm responsible for everyone's safety. We are strangers in a very strange land. We don't even know if we can trust the Junji, let alone the Guild. It's not our struggle, not our fight, and I say we stay out of it."

"But we are Dino Knights," argued Henry. "We protect those who need our help. It's our duty."

"Our duty is to Brecklan," corrected Torin sharply. "And we're only here because of you, Henry. Our quest is to explore the East and discover what happened to your parents, not to interfere in matters we do not understand."

Henry felt torn. He knew the leader of the Dino Knights had a point, but he couldn't turn away when people needed help. It was both his best and worst quality.

"You're right, this isn't our struggle," he said. "But we can't just ignore what has happened to Hannah and her tribe.

Remember, the Junji could have imprisoned us, but instead they're treating us as guests. Surely, we should return the gesture by helping them when they need it most."

Silent until now, Iyla tapped Henry on the shoulder. "I agree with you," she said. "If we don't help, who will?"

Swallowing her hurt pride, Ellie added her support. "Henry, you helped me when my folk were in trouble, so maybe it's time for me to do the same for someone else."

Torin looked over at Gally, who was normally the one to avoid outright conflict. But rather than siding with the leader, he shrugged. "Can't you see Henry's already made up his mind, Torin?" he said. "And we know from last time it's better to stick together than divide the team."

Torin let out a resigned sigh. "We are better together," he declared. "We are the

Dino Knights, and perhaps it is our duty to help the Junji. But we need a plan."

"I can help with that," said Hannah, stepping into the light of the fire. "I didn't mean to listen in, but thank you for lending your swords to our cause."

She held up a wide scroll of parchment paper and let it roll to the ground, revealing a detailed sketch of a tall, castle-like building.

"This is the Guild's outpost," she explained, pointing to an area in the middle of the drawing, "and here's the vault where they're keeping our aqua jewels. There is a rear entrance that's not guarded at night when the soldiers change their shift."

"Then that's where we shall strike," declared Henry..

The Dino Knights set out under cover of darkness.

Hannah rode with Henry, and the team followed her directions. Their path through the desert was lit by millions of stars. Henry had never seen such a huge emptiness, but the night sky offered a vast canvas for the stars to shine.

However, as the group crested a large sand dune, the stars on the horizon were blocked out by an imposing fortress, which suddenly seemed alarmingly close.

"There it is," said Hannah.

The Guild outpost was much larger than Henry had expected. Lit by torches, it was guarded by soldiers holding spears and swords.

"You want us to attack ... that?" asked Torin hesitantly.

In the starlight, Henry could see the building was topped with a flag flapping gently in the night breeze, and he could just about make out its emblem: a sword and fist.

"Wait for it," Hannah said, holding up her hand.

As she had predicted, the soldiers retreated inside to change their shift.

"The next rotation won't be out for a few minutes. Now, we can climb onto your dinos to sneak in through that upper window, and take the jewels out through the back gate."

Henry steered Rex around to the side of the structure and urged Rex to lift himself up like an angled ramp. He scrambled up his dino's neck and used his head like a stepping stone to get onto the ledge.

"Sorry about this, my friend," Henry whispered.

Rex stifled a snort in retort.

Henry peered through the open window but nobody was around. He extended his hand back for Hannah, who followed suit and joined Henry inside the forbidding fortress.

She turned and whispered to the

others. "There's no need for you all to follow us in. We'll unlock the vault, then you can meet us at the back gate and help us fill the sacks."

Once inside, Hannah led Henry along a raised walkway lit by torches. The outpost was built around a huge atrium, open to the starry night sky. Below, Henry spotted the Guild's fleet of six armoured land-boats, each mounted with cannons and harpoon guns; a sleeping armada, just waiting to be woken for war.

"They use those battleships to attack us and hunt the roaming beasts," Hannah explained as they came to a staircase that led them downstairs. Now on the ground floor, they walked past the vessels, keeping close to the walls until they turned into a tall, wide corridor near the back of the building. Hannah led the way to

their destination: a heavy iron door on their right.

"I'll unlock the vault," she whispered. "The back gate is over there on the left – you'd better open it so your friends can come inside to help us."

Hannah fished a collection of small tools out of her pack and expertly tinkered with the lock. For his part, Henry lifted the bar on the rear gate and swung the tall gates open. He guessed this must be where the battleships were moved in and out of the fortress.

"Pssst," called Hannah, beckoning Henry over to the vault, which was open now. Grabbing one of the torches from the wall, he stepped into the dark room.

It took a moment for his eyes to adjust, but myriad sparkling colours were reflected in the torchlight: it was a genuine treasure trove. Having grown up a poor stable boy, Henry had never seen such riches. "Wow," he gasped.

"Gold, jewels, precious metals and sacred objects," Hannah explained. "The Guild takes whatever it wants from whoever it can."

Running into the fortress through the open back gate, the rest of the Dino Knights followed Henry into the vault. The sight before them stopped them in their tracks.

"What happens to all this?" asked Iyla, gaping at the stolen loot.

"The Guild sends a load back east every few months," said Hannah. "There's probably already a transport on its way to move this lot out."

"I thought we were here for aqua jewels," said Torin with a tone of doubt in his voice.

But Hannah was quick to answer. "We take it all to stop the Guild from profiting from their plunder. We can return the stolen loot to its rightful owners across the Dry Lands."

The Dino Knights sprang into action. They unfurled the sacks made from dinosaur hides, and piled in as many treasures as they could. Then they heaved them outside, onto the backs of their waiting dinos.

"You keep watch while Henry and I get one more load. Then we should go," urged Hannah. "The morning shift will be here any minute."

As Henry went back into the vault to help Hannah carry out the last of the sacks, he had an uneasy feeling that something wasn't right. Putting down the heavy sack, he confronted his new friend. "I can't believe they took this much treasure from your people," he said.

Hannah picked up a golden trinket that had fallen onto the floor and placed it in the sack.

"This loot was stolen from all across the Dry Lands," she admitted.

Henry hesitated. This wasn't the plan. They were supposed to reclaim the Junji's stolen aqua jewels so the tribe could start trading again for water. But this was something else. This was a heist.

"I don't know, Hannah," he said, his resolve now wavering.

"No, you don't," she snapped. "You come from a leafy paradise, with clean water and bushes that produce magical berries that tame the beasts. We struggle to survive in a barren desert and face the most brutal foe. You don't know, Henry

Fairchild. You don't know anything!"

Henry stared at her. "I know this is stealing," he countered.

"Stealing from thieves," she answered. "Now let's go!"

"No, I'm not taking this."

As Henry stood his ground, Hannah raced for the door – and slammed it behind her.

"Hannah, no!" he called.

But she bolted the door shut, trapping Henry inside the vault. She opened the peep hole to speak to him.

"I have to do this to look after my people. I'll not have you stop me," Hannah said, justifying her actions. "But I'll tell your friends you've been captured, and I'm sure they'll come back for you."

Henry lowered his head until it bumped on the iron door with a thud.

He was alone in the vault and felt like a fool for trusting Hannah. He slumped down onto the floor, angry with himself. His friends would do the right thing and come back for him, wouldn't they?

After what seemed like forever, Henry heard the bolt open on the other side of the door. With a sigh of relief, he stood to greet the Dino Knights. But when the door opened, he faced the blade of an unfriendly sword.

"You've been caught red-handed, thief," announced an angry soldier, swinging his blade at Henry. This was no play fight at the Friendship Games – this was for real.

Henry drew his sword and parried in defence, pushing his way out of the door. His opponent was strong, but Henry was fast.

They duelled backwards along the corridor and into the grand atrium. The night sky above was giving way to dawn. In the early morning light, Henry got the full measure of his foe. Dressed in red military uniform, his chest was decorated with colourful pins to mark victory in battle. On his left arm, he wore the sword and fist emblem that Henry had spotted earlier on the flag.

"You fight well, boy," said the man, wiping sweat from his brow. But soldiers were moving in to surround the atrium – there was no escape. Fighting between the land-ships, Henry was tiring, and his enemy was relentless.

"Surrender now, and I'll spare your life," his opponent offered.

"Captain Carey!" one of the soldiers called out. "The vault has been cleared out!"

The expression on Carey's face changed from annoyance to fear. Henry realised this man answered to powerful people: the missing treasure was a matter of life or death for him.

"What have you done, you Junji snake?!" Carey cried.

"I'm not Junji," replied Henry. "My name is Henry Fairchild, and I'm a Dino Knight of Brecklan."

Carey sneered. "Never heard of you, but the Guild will crush you along with all who stand in our way. We expand ever westwards and know no bounds."

As the other soldiers moved closer, Carey toyed with Henry with jabs of his sword.

"Tell me, boy," he said. "How did you get mixed up with the Junji?"

"I was helping them take back their aqua jewels, so they could survive in the desert."

Carey laughed. "Ah, the damsel-in-distress trick. You actually fell for it?"

Henry didn't like being laughed at, but he knew this Captain Carey wasn't wrong: Hannah had used the Dino Knights to help her steal other people's treasure.

"The Junji are conniving sand pirates," Carey explained. "They roam the Dry Lands, pilfering what they want and moving on. Only the Guild can bring peace and order to this lawless land."

Suddenly, someone grabbed Henry from behind, hoisting him into the air. His sword dropped with a clank as his arm was yanked behind his back in an armlock.

"It's over, Henry Fairchild," said Carey. "You fought bravely, but you should never have come here."

"What should we do with him?" asked the soldier holding Henry.

"Toss him in the dungeon with the beast-huggers while we decide his fate."

The soldiers led Henry to another iron door, unlocked it and shoved him over the threshold. As the door closed behind him, Henry staggered towards a staircase. Carefully, he felt his way down until he reached a hard floor. The dungeon was dark, lit only by a small barred window set high in the wall.

"Who's that?" a woman asked in the gloom.

"Someone who's upset the Guild," replied a man.

"Hello," Henry said timidly. "Who's there?"

"The monsters!" cried the woman. "They've captured a child."

"I'm not a child," Henry replied with what remained of his pride. "I am Henry Fairchild of the Dino Knights of Brecklan."

There was a long silence.

"Sylvia ... it ... it ... can't be," whispered the man.

"Harris, he said *Henry Fairchild*!" cried the woman. "Our baby ... but ... we lost him so many years ago ..."

As Henry's eyes adjusted to the dark, he could just make out the faces of his fellow prisoners. He recognised them from his dreams.

"Mum? Dad?"

VII

For the first time since he could remember, Henry felt the warm embrace of his parents. He could feel their love and longing, and despite being in this awful place, Henry never wanted their hug to end.

"We thought we'd lost you that terrible day," said Harris, his father.

"I feared I'd never hold you again," added Sylvia, the mother Henry had never known.

For his part, Henry could not believe he was with them at last. He too had longed to be reunited, but despite many dreams, and sometimes nightmares, he had only ever had a faint hope he might discover his parents' fate. He had never actually expected to meet them.

But now, here they all were together again, yet trapped in a dungeon by an evil force bent on relentless expansion. What should have been a happy reunion was overshadowed by a sense of dread. But Henry had one burning question for his parents.

"Why ... why did you abandon me?"

"My darling Henry," cried Sylvia. "It wasn't like that at all. We came under attack and hid you in a cave to keep you safe. But when we returned ..."

She could not finish her sentence.

"It's all right, Sylvia," Harris said softly. "We've found him now." He turned to his son, taking his hand.

"Son, we set out on King Rannick's request, to explore these lands and try to build bridges with the rest of Panterra, but we soon discovered we weren't the only pioneers in this unforgiving desert. Soldiers from the east had come here to slaughter the dinosaurs. They call themselves the Guild. Their plan is to clear these lands, so the people who are crammed into their cities can move west. But to do this, the Guild need to get rid of the dinosaurs, along with the tribes that call the Dry Lands home. We tried to stop the Guild, but they attacked our expedition – we couldn't risk you getting hurt, so we hid you from harm."

His mother wiped away tears from her dirt-streaked face. "We came back to the cave after the attack, but you had disappeared," she sniffed. "We never stopped looking for you, Henry. As we searched, we lived among the Dry Landers and learnt their ways, even while we carried on fighting the Guild. But one day, we got caught."

"How long have you been down here?" Henry asked.

"We've stopped counting," his father replied grimly.

Henry tried to take it all in. He had grown up in Brecklan and thrived as a Dino Knight, while his parents had been locked away in this dank dungeon. Henry felt sick at the injustice of it all.

He tried to blink back the tears but failed.

"All this time," he wept. "It's just so unfair."

His mother held him tightly. "But we're together now. Let's focus on that."

Henry was exhausted from the trek across the mountains, the encounter with the Junji, and his sword fight in the fortress. His heart was heavy and his whole body ached. Now that he'd found his parents, the sense of relief drained him completely.

His mother laid him down gently on a makeshift bed of straw.

"You should rest, Henry," his father whispered.

Sylvia stroked Henry's hair as his eyes closed. "There's a lullaby I used to sing to you when you were a baby," she said. "Perhaps it will comfort you now, as it did then."

She began to sing, softly.

*"Hush now, little one,
There's no need for fear.
You are loved, you are dear;
The world is wide but our love is true.
We will always be in your heart,
   and never leave you."*

Henry drifted off to the sound of his mother's voice. At once, he was somewhere different. He was back in Brecklan, in a small house he didn't recognise, but somehow felt was his home. He breathed in the smell of breakfast cooking. In the kitchen, his father was frying eggs, while his mother was feeding a small pet Triceratops.

"Time for breakfast before school?" asked Harris.

"Most important meal of the day," said Sylvia, as Henry patted the Triceratops.

The scene seemed so normal, but was a slice of life that Henry had never actually known. It was perfect, but it wasn't real.

And at once, Henry woke from the dream. He was still in the dungeon, but the iron door at the top of the stairs was clanking open.

"Boy!" called a stern soldier's voice. "Captain Carey wants to see you."

Henry rose drowsily to his feet. His father put his hands on his shoulders.

"Son, be careful," he warned. "Don't believe everything Carey tells you. He isn't loyal to the Guild, or to anyone else. All he really cares about is getting his family to the Oasis."

"The what?" asked Henry.

"It's where the Guild promises to send their best soldiers," explained Sylvia.

"But we discovered it's a lie," added Harris. "The Oasis doesn't even exist. The Guild dangles the prospect of a perfect life to get soldiers to do their bidding. But when the poor fools and their families are packed off there, they're actually sent into exile, because they're considered no longer useful. It's cruel, but that's the Guild for you."

"How do you know so much?" Henry asked.

"We may have been locked away," said his father, "but we've been paying attention."

"And we've been planning," added his mother.

"Hurry, boy!" barked the soldier's voice. "Captain Carey does not like to be kept waiting."

"Go," urged Henry's mother. "But give nothing away. Listen and learn. The Guild may be inhumane, but it is not invincible."

Henry moved towards the stairs and climbed them slowly. He knew he had to be both smart and careful. His life, and the lives of his parents, depended on it.

VIII

The soldier led Henry up to a large banqueting hall that overlooked the expansive desert beyond the fortress walls.

"Impressive, isn't it?" said Captain Carey, as Henry entered.

The Guild captain was at the head of a huge wooden table that could easily seat thirty people. He gestured for Henry to take the place beside him. Henry stared at the large plates laden with food for the taking: scrambled eggs, warm bread and fresh fruit. His stomach rumbled – it had been a long time since his last meal.

Seeing the hunger on Henry's face, Carey urged his prisoner to eat.

Henry filled his plate as Carey lifted a goblet of steaming liquid to his lips and sipped.

"I remember when I first came here," Carey began. "I had never seen so much space. I would stand there by that window, just looking out towards the horizon. There was so much … well, nothing. A void, waiting to be filled." Carey took another sip of his drink. "Where I come from, the city is packed with people. On some streets, you can barely move for the crowds. And yet here, there's space for everyone. But this desert is dangerous, with rampaging beasts and roaming people who think they have a claim to the land. The Guild needs to purge the desert of these threats to make space for our kind, our future. We must build homes for everyone stuck in the city like caged animals. That's why I'm here, to prepare for the Great Resettlement."

He put down his goblet and looked Henry in the eye.

"But I need to know something. Why are *you* here?"

The Dino Knight didn't want to reveal too much, but he didn't want to lie either.

"I have come from the west, across the mountain range, seeking a new land to explore," he replied carefully.

"And treasure to plunder?" snapped

Carey. "You were caught helping the Junji to steal from me."

"But you steal from *them*," Henry replied.

Carey nodded, not attempting to deny the charge. "For good reason," he replied. "I have orders to send treasure back to the Guild every month. If I don't obey those orders, I will be replaced and then my family..."

He stopped short. Suddenly and unexpectedly, Henry sensed fear in Captain Carey's voice. He clearly needed to do his masters' bidding, or something bad would happen. But the captain quickly masked his emotion.

"To secure the treasure," he continued, "I need good fighters."

"You seem to have a lot of soldiers here," Henry observed.

"Quantity is not the same as quality," Carey replied. "My soldiers are conscripts, forced to serve out here as Guild guards. They have no spirit or fire in their hearts. But you, boy, you have both spirit and fire. When we crossed swords, I could tell you have something none of my soldiers possess."

"What's that?" Henry asked.

"Purpose. Belief. You fight for something bigger than yourself." He stood up from the table. "And that's why I am offering you a place at my side."

Henry was taken aback. Was this man trying to recruit him? He remembered his father's warning – could Carey be trusted?

"If you join me," continued Carey, "I can bring you into the Guild and promise you a place in paradise."

"You mean, the Oasis?" asked Henry.

"How do you know about that?" he snapped.

Before Henry could answer, the door swung open.

"I said I was not to be disturbed!" barked the captain.

But his face transformed from fury to fondness as a young boy, no more than four years old, ran towards him holding a toy dinosaur.

"Daddy!" the boy cried excitedly. A young woman was chasing after him.

"I'm so sorry, Carey, dear," she panted, out of breath. "I've been trying to keep Hunter out of here, but he insisted on seeing your beast-rider for himself!"

"My what?" said Carey.

"Him!" replied the boy, pointing to Henry. "I saw him yesterday, riding on the back of a big beast."

"You must've been imagining things again, Hunter," said Carey, picking up his son. He frowned at his wife. "Bella, you mustn't fill our boy's head with such silly ideas."

She took Hunter back to carry him out of the room, but Henry stopped them both.

"It's true," he said to the boy. "My beast is a kind of dinosaur called a T-Rex. He's a mighty theropod, which means he walks on two back legs. He's a fierce meat-eater, but with me, he's gentle and loyal. Believe me, Hunter, riding a dinosaur is the most amazing thing."

"Wow," said the boy, his mouth open in awe.

"Nonsense!" dismissed Captain Carey. "These beasts are wild and cannot be tamed."

Henry stood his ground, facing up to Carey. "And yet I come from a place where we live side by side with dinosaurs, and they are part of our lives. It's our Oasis. And it's *real.*"

Doubt flickered across the captain's face. "But what do you know about our Oasis?" he asked.

"I know it's not real," Henry replied. "It's just a fiction created by the Guild to get people like you to do what they want. Have you ever seen this Oasis?"

"What's he talking about, Carey?" asked Bella, her voice trembling.

Carey did not answer, but Henry could tell he must have already had doubts, and was beginning to wonder whether the thing he placed so much faith in was no more real than a mirage in the desert.

"But if you free the two prisoners from

your dungeon, I can lead you and your family to a real place of peace and plenty," Henry persisted. "A place where Hunter can grow up to ride dinosaurs. A place called Brecklan."

The boy's eyes widened at this. "Mummy! Daddy! I want to ride dinosaurs!" he cried.

Bella narrowed her eyes at her husband. "You told me there was no one left down in that dungeon."

The captain shuffled uncomfortably, looking at the floor and then back to his wife. He had clearly been caught out in a lie.

"Please, Bella, you have to understand, I couldn't free those two beast-huggers. They would have made life impossible for us. They would have tried to block the Great Resettlement, which would have stopped us from getting to the Oasis."

Bella was angry, but before she could reply, a strange sound like a horn filled the room.

"A herald!" whooped Hunter, clapping his hands.

Carey rushed over to the window. Henry, Bella and Hunter joined him to see a man standing below wearing a red uniform, holding a brass trumpet that reflected the dazzling sun. He stood beside a solo land-boat.

"I have a command from the Guild," the herald announced.

Carey looked worried that it would be bad news. "We'd better hear what he has to say," he sighed.

Henry went down with the family to meet the herald outside the front gates of the fortress.

"What is your message?" Carey asked.

"The Guild has run out of patience," the herald replied. "You have not made enough progress at this outpost. An army is on its way to finish what you failed to complete: the final clearing of beasts from this territory, so the Great Resettlement can begin. Prepare this fortress for the arrival of the army. It will become the launching point for the extinction of the beasts."

"No!" cried Hunter. "Don't kill the dinosaurs!"

"Silence your brat," hissed the herald.

"Speak not of my son," snapped Carey. "We have made progress here despite difficult conditions. But there are too many beasts, and the tribes are too tethered to their traditions. We just need more time."

The herald shrugged. "That is the one thing you do not have, Captain," he said. "You have failed here, and you and your family will answer for this."

Carey tried to hide his panic. "What about the Oasis?" he asked. "My family was promised a place there if we came to this outpost."

But the herald just laughed. "You fool," he sneered. "The Oasis isn't real, it's just something the Guild tells gullible soldiers to keep them motivated."

Carey flashed Henry a look of despair. For the first time since meeting him, Henry saw that the captain was lost for words.

"Now, out of my way," ordered the herald. "I've been crossing the desert for days and require a bath and a meal."

He pushed past them as if he owned the place and disappeared inside.

Hunter began to cry. "Don't let them kill the dinosaurs, Daddy," he begged.

Bella looked bewildered. Henry realised the captain did not want to disappoint his family, but could not risk angering the almighty Guild, which was on the march.

"Captain Carey," Henry began. "You pulled me out of the dungeon this morning to recruit me to your cause. But now I'm going to recruit you to mine: the defence of the dinosaurs. These great creatures do not deserve extinction."

"But man and beast cannot live together," argued Carey, still doubtful.

"I used to think that too," called a familiar voice.

A lasso whipped through the air from around the corner and looped around Carey's chest. Hannah followed, confidently astride Rex, and she tugged the captain across the sand towards her.

"Let my daddy go!" cried Hunter, staring at the dinosaur and his rider.

"Don't worry, Hunter, that's my dino!" Henry reassured him. "You won't hurt this little boy's father, will you, Rex?"

Henry's dino snorted, and held his ground, as the other Dino Knights rounded the corner of the fortress.

"I'm sorry about last night, Henry," called Hannah. "Your Dino Knights convinced me I was wrong about taking all that treasure. We've all come back here to rescue you."

Henry walked towards Rex to give him a stroke. "Thank you, Hannah, for changing your mind," he said, then turned to his friends. "And it's so good to see you all again! But I think Captain Carey here is about to have a change of heart too."

Henry reached down to help the captain to his feet.

"You see, we *can* live with the dinosaurs," the Dino Knight explained to him. "Where I come from, we ride them. But right now, it's not me who needs saving, it's all the dinosaurs of the Dry Lands. I'm going to untie you Captain Carey, but only if you agree to save the dinosaurs from extinction."

The Captain looked at his family and then locked eyes with Henry, nodding his head to confirm his commitment to Henry's cause.

A heavily armed platoon of Guild guards rushed to the front gates, ready to fend off the Dino Knights. But Captain Carey, now free from the lasso, stood them down with a shake of his head.

"I think we ought to listen to what this young knight has to say," Carey told his men.

Henry stood beside Rex and addressed the assembled soldiers. He knew he had to win their hearts and minds to commit them to his cause.

"I know you feel like you're doing what is right out here. You've travelled far to create a place for your people to flourish in the desert, but there is another way. A way you can live alongside dinosaurs. We have learnt how to do it in my homeland – we use special berries to tame our 'beasts'. And we can share this crop with you, so that you can ride dinosaurs as we do. But first, you have to combine forces with us, to stop the Guild army that is marching here as I speak to kill these amazing creatures."

Some of the soldiers muttered musings about risking their chance to reach the Oasis.

"It's not real, my friends," Carey stated. "We have been lied to for too long, promised nothing more than a mirage."

The soldiers scoffed in disbelief. But like Carey, Henry suspected that many of them knew deep down that it was too good to be true.

"If you want to live in an oasis, it's up to you to create one," said Henry.

There was a ripple of reluctant approval from the soldiers.

Carey stepped forward to join Henry. "We will stand with you," he said. "And we will fight with you."

The soldiers saluted their captain to demonstrate their loyalty, but one of them spoke up to reveal what they were all thinking. "We are few, Captain, to stand against a whole army," he said.

Hannah climbed off Rex to join

Henry's side. "Actually, there are more of us than you think," she said. "My Junji tribe will help you repel this horde. And I believe the other tribes of the Dry Lands will join your cause, but they will need to be persuaded by someone they trust."

Henry knew the answer to this problem: his parents. They had spent years working with many tribes in the Dry Lands to protect the dinosaurs before they had been captured by the Guild.

"I know who could help with that," Henry said to Hannah, before turning to his friends. "My parents! I found them! They're in prison here, in the dungeon of this fortress, but if Captain Carey will grant their freedom, they would be the ones to recruit more desert tribes to our cause."

"I'm so happy you found them at last, Henry," said Ellie, tears in her eyes.

Captain Carey looked to his Guild guards, who were depending on him for leadership. "Release the prisoners at once!" he ordered.

Henry went with the guards to the dungeon, and when they unlocked the door, he ran down the stairs to liberate his parents.

"Mum! Dad!" he called.

"What's happening?" asked his mother.

"Captain Carey is letting you go," Henry replied. "But we're not free, not yet. A huge Guild army is marching towards this fortress, with orders to kill all the dinosaurs."

"They're evil," declared his father.

"And determined," added Henry. "And we have to stop them. But we're going to need help, and that's where you both come in."

Henry led his parents to the main atrium. The Dino Knights, Hannah, and Carey's guards were already beginning to move the land-ships out of the back gate, to assemble the fleet for battle. But even if Sylvia and Harris could convince other desert tribes to join the cause – and fast – they would still be outnumbered by the approaching Guild army.

That's when Henry had an idea. Lord Harding had been trying to bring together the different realms of western Panterra to work alongside each other. Perhaps if Henry could get word to Harding, he could rally Brecklan and the neighbouring provinces to the battle. That might just tip the scales in their favour.

Henry asked Carey for some parchment and quickly penned a plea for help to his master. Rolling the message up into a scroll, he secured it with some twine. Without stopping to explain himself, he raced up to the roof of the fortress.

Squinting at the wide, desert sky, Henry cupped his hands to his mouth and made the call of a pterosaur. His parents followed closely behind to find their long-lost son bellowing into the hot breeze.

"Wh-wh-what are you doing?" Harris panted, out of breath from so much time in captivity.

"Something I learnt from a battle," Henry replied, thinking of the time he had once called for a pterosaur in the Swamp States, before riding home to Brecklan.

"You've been in a battle?" asked his mother.

"A few," Henry admitted. There were so many stories he needed to tell them, but now was not the time.

He tried the pterosaur call again, but only silence called back. Finally, he cleared his mind and conjured up an image: he pictured a flock of pterosaurs and made the call as loudly as he could.

At first, there was still nothing, and Henry's heart sank with desperation. But then, he heard the distant flap of wings. Soon, he saw it: a young pterosaur breaking off from its flock. It flew towards him and his parents, landing on a turret.

"Incredible," gasped Sylvia. "He can talk to them, Harris."

Henry placed his hands on the creature's beak and closed his eyes. He had a way of communicating with dinosaurs and pterosaurs that even he didn't understand, but it was a type of deep connection. In his mind, he pictured Harding Manor, and asked the pterosaur to

fly over the mountains to take the scroll to his master, Lord Harding.

At first, the pterosaur seemed reluctant.

"I know you can do it," Henry urged. "It is far, but you are strong."

The pterosaur responded with a low chirp. Henry tied the scroll with his message around the creature's left foot. With a gentle pat, he encouraged it to fly.

Unfurling its massive wings, the pterosaur glided off the turret, up into the sky. And just as Henry had hoped for, it banked west and flew towards the mountains that separated the Dry Lands from Brecklan.

"You have a gift," Sylvia said in awe.

"Well, I used to be a stable boy," Henry explained. "I suppose I just sort of developed a way with them."

"It's so much more than that," observed his father.

"Henry," his mother continued, "when we returned to that cave to find you, we found an empty dinosaur nest. The animal must have thought its nest had been disturbed by us, and gone to build another somewhere else. I wonder now if you might have been taken by that dinosaur, and reared alongside its offspring."

Henry had no memory of this, but he had dreamt about being among hatching dinosaur eggs before. Did dinosaurs consider him to be one of their own? It would explain so much about his connection to them.

Lord Harding had never told him exactly how he'd come to Harding Manor, but had recounted a legend about a boy raised as a dinosaur, and he'd also described finding the young Henry playing with a flock of raptors.

Henry still had so many questions about his childhood, but right now he needed to prepare for battle. A war was looming, and unless Henry could assemble a force to confront the Guild army, the dinosaurs of the Dry Lands would be lost forever. And Henry knew that would just be the beginning. Over time, the Guild would scale the mountains and come for Brecklan too.

Henry had to stop the Guild now, or everything he loved would be lost.

Riding on Rex with Hannah, flanked by Captain Carey's fleet, Henry led the Dino Knights and his parents back to the Junji encampment.

At first, Hera was appalled to see a Guild captain approaching her tribe, shoulder to shoulder with Henry, her daughter's new friend.

"You dare bring our enemy here?" she snarled at the Dino Knight.

Henry attempted to channel Lord Harding's gift for diplomacy. "We are facing a threat bigger than all of us put together," he explained, pointing to the battleships behind him. "Captain Carey commands this fleet, but no longer for the Guild. He now fights for the good of the dinosaurs and the people of the Dry Lands."

"He is making amends for being a cog in a terrible machine," added Torin. "One that is now marching across the desert, to get here in two days' time."

Captain Carey bowed his head as a sign of respect to the tribal leader. "I know I've wronged you and your people in the past, Elder Hera," he confessed. "But Henry has shown me a new path forwards, where my people can live in harmony with the land and its animals ... and the tribes that care for both."

Hera considered the captain's words, but was more persuaded by his actions.

"You are taking up your sword against your own people to protect these lands, so I will fight alongside you," she declared.

Henry breathed a sigh of relief. But he also needed to boost their numbers, so he and Hannah instructed the Junji to round up any dinosaurs roaming near the encampment, and to bring them in to feed from the supply of Brecklan Berries the Dino Knights carried with them. One by one, the Junji brought dinos into the camp for Henry to train. As with the pterosaur back at the fortress, Henry asked each one to ride into battle with the Junji against the coming Guild army. The combination of his empathetic connection and the taming power of the berries allowed the Junji to enlist a large brigade of dinosaurs.

Hannah chose a Pachycephalosaurus to ride into battle – a theropod with a domed head that looked as if it could knock through a stone wall. She named it Nikki, after a wild, feathered Stenonychosaurus she had once tried to keep as a pet, until it broke out of its pen and ran away.

Henry's parents selected a matching pair of Parasaurolophuses to ride. They reminded Henry of Lord Harding's carriage bearers, which seemed a good omen.

Torin reviewed battle tactics with their new allies, whilst Iyla outfitted them with new weapons. Ellie and Gally ran a makeshift riding school, teaching the Junji the basics of how to ride dinosaurs into battle.

Once the Junji had assembled their cavalry of dinos, Henry rode out with his parents to find more tribes to recruit. Everything depended on the success of this mission.

They cantered across the Dry Lands to meet the Nerain, the Cetwa, and the Osauga tribes. At first, each tribe met Henry with suspicion, but then recognised Sylvia and Harris from their work with dinosaurs many years before. The leader of the Cetwa, a young man called Grythor, recognised Henry's parents and embraced them warmly. "I remember you from when I was a boy," he said. "You learnt our ways and taught us yours. Now I'm leader of my tribe, I will join you."

Henry was proud of his parents. He marvelled at how good deeds of the past were now paying dividends. It was a lesson he never wanted to forget.

As Henry, Harris and Sylvia travelled

around the tribes, giving them Brecklan Berries to tame nearby dinos, the forces they'd already gathered assembled at Carey's fortress.

There were hundreds of willing soldiers now, with dinosaur brigades and half a dozen battleships. But Henry was still worried it would not be enough to stop the incoming army. A scout riding a fast raptor arrived at the fortress to confirm his fears.

"I rode here as fast as I could," the young lad reported. "The Guild army is huge, easily a thousand strong. They are moving in a massive column backed by land-battleships and catapult towers."

"That is the Guild way," explained Captain Carey. "To overwhelm the enemy with sheer numbers and firepower."

"But we have dino power," Henry replied. "And incentive. The Junji, the

Cetwa, the Nerain and the Osauga are fighting for the land they live on."

"Hopefully that will be enough," said Gally, unhelpfully.

"Hope is not a strategy," replied Torin, repeating a mantra that Harding had tried to teach them.

Henry, Carey, Hannah and the Dino Knights began drawing up a battle plan. Iyla suggested they use the desert terrain to their advantage. "We could dig wide trenches in the ground to stop the army getting into the fortress," she said.

"Like a dry moat," agreed Ellie. "And we could leap over the trenches on our dinos, to launch the counter-attack."

"And if we move the land-ships out before the Guild army gets close, we can hide them behind the sand dunes for a surprise attack," said Torin.

Even Gally added to the plan. "But let's construct catapults up on the battlements, just in case they do get within range."

They mobilised quickly. Some of Carey's soldiers beat shields from their land-boats into ploughs, which they then harnessed to dinosaurs. Other soldiers moved the fortress' fleet behind the sand dunes. As the ploughs carved the trenches into the ground, they created a barrier that the Guild's battleships could not cross without getting stuck.

Meanwhile, Henry caught a roaming Allosaurus and tamed her. Captain Carey took to the dino instantly, calling her Ally. With Henry's help, he quickly learnt how to ride the bipodal carnivore.

"You're a natural," Henry said.

"I could get used to this," Carey said with a smile.

By the time the trenches had all been dug, the sun was setting over the mountains. Henry and Carey sat on their dinosaurs by the fortress gates, scanning the horizon as the day ended.

"Do you think the Guild would listen to reason?" Henry asked.

The captain shook his head. "Probably not, but it's worth a try," he replied.

Carey's soldiers had put down a temporary bridge across the trench for Henry and Carey to ride over. So as dusk turned to night, the pair left the safety of the fortress to venture east towards the incoming army and attempt a parley. The rest of the Dino Knights and Carey's forces would be close behind in case the Guild wasn't in any mood to talk.

Walk softly and carry a big axe, thought Henry. Ellie's uncle would have been proud.

As they got closer, the front of the marching column came into view. Henry saw a banner held high, with the Guild's sword and fist emblem visible by the light of a flaming torch. These were a proud people, and Henry suspected they would not back down easily.

"Company, halt!" shouted a Guild soldier upon spotting Henry and Carey.

The column, ready for war, came to a reluctant standstill. Henry counted at least fifteen land-boats and battleships, and many wooden catapult towers on wheels. The dry air buzzed with tension.

"Who stands in our way?" called a grizzled voice.

"Uh oh," whispered Carey. "I know that voice. It's General Razzath, my instructor at the Guild Academy. He's as fierce as he is cruel." He stood tall to confront

his old teacher. "General Razzath," Carey called out. "It's me, sir. Cadet— I mean, *Captain* Carey."

The general walked to the front of the column to greet his former student. They each punched the fists of their right hand into the palms of their left – a Guild greeting.

"Carey! I see you've learnt a new trick out here in the desert," Razzath said, prodding Ally, who snorted angrily.

"I have learnt a lot more than dino-riding, sir," Carey replied, nodding at his old master.

Razzath sniffed. "But I understand that you have failed in your mission here," he said with contempt. "What a disappointment you turned out to be, Cadet Carey, after all your training with me. Your last duty will be to lead me to your fortress, so we can take over from your incompetence and clear these lands for the Great Resettlement."

Carey managed to keep his cool at this insult. "I'm not here to assist you," he replied, "but to warn you. You must leave now, and take the Guild army back to the east."

The general tensed into a fighting stance. "You dare to defy orders and betray your people?" he hissed.

Henry spoke up to defend his ally. "He betrays no one, General Razzath. The Guild are misguided in their pursuits out here. Captain Carey wants to stop any bloodshed before it's too late."

"This boy speaks for you?!" Razzath spat.

Again, Carey remained calm. "This young man, Henry Fairchild, has opened my eyes to what is possible when we live *with* the land and don't try to conquer it."

Razzath shot him a contemptuous look. "You have forgotten everyone you left behind in the city, Carey. Life there has got worse: it's crowded, diseased and dangerous. We are here to give our people a new start, and yet you and this *fair child* stand in our way. You are a traitor and you will answer for your disloyalty. But only after I personally oversee the clearing of the Dry Lands for our people to settle here."

"I won't let that happen," said Henry, reaching for his sword.

But Razzath mocked the young fighter. "You and what army, boy?" he jeered.

"This one," replied Henry. "The Dino Knights!"

On cue, the four Dino Knights thundered out of the darkness, followed by Hannah, the Junji and the united Dry Landers.

The battle had begun.

XI

Henry raised his sword and Rex unleashed an almighty roar.

Razzath ordered the Guild army to attack, charging forward with swords and spears. But Iyla turned Conker around to swipe his tail at the rushing forces, knocking the first of them aside like skittles.

Razzath climbed aboard one of the land-battleships and ordered his fleet to launch harpoons. Sharp-tipped spears soared overhead and struck some of the dinosaurs.

Henry manoeuvred Rex to push Nikki out of the way of an incoming harpoon.

"That was close," gasped Hannah.

Carey ordered his fleet of battleships to attack from behind the sand dunes. They navigated across the sand to flank the Guild's fleet, and trained their cannons on the enemy ships. With deafening bangs, the warring vessels traded cannon fire.

More harpoons whizzed through the air. It was an all-out assault, and though the Dino Knights had assembled a great battalion of fighters and dinos, the Guild simply had strength in numbers and began to advance.

"Fall back! To the trenches!" Carey ordered.

The Dry Lander allies retreated to positions on the fortress side of the grand trench.

"This will frustrate their advance," Carey assured Henry, who was concerned about being so badly outnumbered.

And for a few minutes, it did slow the assault. The Guild army had to stop at the trench, because their battleships and catapults could not pass over it. But, undeterred, soldiers began to lay planks over the trenches to make temporary bridges, so their equipment and vehicles could cross.

Henry waited until the first bridge was assembled, then rode Rex back into the trench to crouch underneath it. As soon as a catapult trundled over the bridge,

Henry signalled to Rex to rear up on his back legs.

"As high as you can, Rex!" called Henry.

The T-Rex stood tall and headbutted the planks of the makeshift bridge to make it fall into the trench. With it, the catapult crashed down, narrowly missing the dino and his rider.

"Nice move, Breck-boy!" Hannah laughed, as she guided Nikki over the trench to take on another land-boat. Nikki rammed her domed head into the front axle of the attacking ship and it careered into the chasm.

That was two down, but Henry couldn't celebrate because he knew the other temporary bridges were still operational, letting battleships and weapons across.

Henry led Rex out of the trench to rejoin the allies at the fortress. Carey and

Torin had assembled the fighters and their dinos into platoons, attacking the battleships on separate fronts. But the Guild's catapults had started to launch fireballs into the sky, landing amid the allied forces. It was all out war.

Between the harpoons and fireballs, the Guild army was advancing too fast for Henry's liking. But the Dry Landers fought back bravely while the Junji fighters rode their dinos with skill, attacking with spears and nets to trap the advancing soldiers. But Henry was sad to see so many dinos struck down by harpoons. He winced as a fireball slammed into a Deinonychus, knocking Grythor off its feathered back. Ellie rushed over on Kayla to pull the young fighter up onto her dinosaur.

In the mayhem of battle, Captain Carey found Henry and insisted their forces fall back to the fortress – at least they could defend their positions from the tall turrets. Carey called for a second retreat and the Dry Landers circled back, putting distance between themselves and the invading army.

"We'll give you cover," Henry offered. He led the Dino Knights and Hannah to attack the lead battleship, giving Carey and the others time to retreat. The knights worked together with Hannah to charge their dinosaurs into the port side of the ship's wooden hull. The combined force of the six dinos lifted the vessel off the ground, its large wheels spinning uselessly in the air.

"One final push!" called Henry.

Conker swung her tail whilst Haringey hurled himself at the wooden hull. Rex rammed into the battleship, tipping it over to lie defenceless in the sand.

The Dino Knights cheered.

"Great work, everyone!" Henry shouted.

The Dry Landers took up positions on the battlements. Henry spotted Captain Carey up there, preparing one of the catapults.

"Fire!" shouted the captain, and four of the catapults launched at once, swinging large boulders through the air. One landed on the deck of a battleship, smashing it in half. The deluge of falling rocks caused the invading army to scramble.

But the Guild forces soon regrouped, aiming back at the Dry Landers with their own wheeled catapults. Large fireballs slammed into the walls of the fortress. Henry wasn't sure how long they could withstand this level of attack.

Hannah raced Nikki straight at one of the enemy catapults, toppling it with one ram of the dino's hard head. But a harpoon whizzed through the air and lodged into Nikki's hind leg. The dinosaur roared in pain and fell to the ground, throwing Hannah off.

Henry rode over and helped Hannah onto Rex's back. "We'll come back for her later," he promised.

Meanwhile, Torin, Ellie and Iyla followed Hannah's lead, steering their dinos into the catapult towers to overturn them. Gally's dinosaur, Avin, was too small to do such damage, but was fast enough to be disruptive. Carrying his rider at top speed, he zipped around the advancing army, nipping and screeching at the soldiers to cause maximum confusion. Gally swung his sword as Avin sped along, knocking down as many enemy fighters as he could.

But even this wasn't enough. Despite the Dino Knights' brave attack, and the barrage of rocks raining down from the fortress, the Guild army was simply too massive for the Dry Landers to repel. Henry knew it was just a matter of time before the Guild overwhelmed the fortress and beat the Dry Landers into submission, before moving on to clear the lands for their so-called Great Resettlement.

Hannah sensed Henry's despondency. "Is this it, then?" she asked, beginning to lose hope.

"I'm not giving up," replied Henry, silently fearing their best efforts might come to nothing.

Then, over the sounds of battle, Henry heard a screech from the air. He looked up to see a pterosaur approaching from the west.

XII

"We heard you could use a hand," called a familiar voice from the sky. "Or a wing."

It was Cylis, the boy Henry had clashed with at the Friendship Games. He was flanked by a squadron of pterosaurs in attack formation, piloted by Swamp States fighters.

Henry's message had been received! And he couldn't be happier to see his old adversary.

"Harding and the rest of our allies are close behind," Cylis added. "But I thought you might need some air support, Henry Actually!"

The pterosaurs dived through the battleships' sails, halting the enemy advance. They knocked over the remaining catapults and snatched up terrified Guild soldiers in their giant beaks, before tossing them back onto the sand below.

The Dino Knights raced over to Henry, who was quick to explain their change of fortune.

"I sent Lord Harding a call for help but didn't think it would be answered so fast!" he cried.

The ground began to shake, and they looked over to see a massive stampede of dinosaurs, mounted by riders and heading towards them. Lord Harding and his cavalry had arrived, just in time.

Now, the Guild army was in disarray, unable to defend itself against the surprise aerial assault. As the land forces arrived, the once mighty army was totally overwhelmed.

Harding rode his Parasaurolophus alongside the other leaders of western Panterra. He had united his former foes to form an overpowering show of strength.

"We came as soon as we could," Harding exclaimed. "All of us."

The Dry Landers emerged from the fortress and joined forces with the new arrivals. Together, they fought back the Guild army until every one of the enemy battleships and catapults had been destroyed.

The Junji tended to the wounded dinosaurs and used their herding skills to round up the prisoners of war and hold them in place until a decision was made about what to do with them. Carey came down from the battlements to join the victorious defenders.

"Razzath," he said, addressing the captured general. "You have been defeated. We will let you and your fellow prisoners go free if you promise to go back to the city and never return. Leave us here in peace."

"You fool," spat Razzath. "If I go back, they'll just send another general and another army – a bigger one. The Guild will expand here whatever you do. It's inevitable."

Hera spoke up. "Captain Carey, listen to me. I know what these people are like. We can't let them leave. They have to die!"

"No, Mother!" cried Hannah. "We've defended our lands. There's no need for more violence today."

"But what about the days that follow?" Hera asked.

"General Razzath is right," said Captain Carey. "And so are you, Hera. The Guild will keep coming. This is just a temporary victory, but it does buy us time."

"But then we would just be living on constant alert," insisted Hera.

Henry's mother Sylvia stepped forward to make a suggestion. "Captain Carey, you switched your allegiance when Henry showed you a new path. Perhaps my son can convince the defeated Guild army to do the same?"

Considering this, Carey nodded at Henry. So the Dino Knight climbed onto a downed catapult tower to address the captured soldiers.

"You have seen today how humans and dinosaurs can live together," he began. "We offer you a choice: to stay here in the Dry Lands to defend the freedom and dignity of the people and animals here, or to march home to face the Guild for your failure. If you wish to start a new life out here in the desert and pledge to defend these lands against the Guild, raise your hand and be counted."

One by one, the prisoners of war lifted their hands to pledge allegiance to their former enemy. Henry had recruited a legion of new allies to defend the Dry Lands.

But Razzath refused to join them.

"We've made the dungeon ready for

you," said Harris, Henry's father. With that, Razzath was hauled into the fortress, to be locked away.

Captain Carey turned to Henry's parents. "I'm so sorry for imprisoning you both for so long. It wasn't until I met your son that I realised how wrong I'd been. I now beg your forgiveness."

Sylvia placed her hand on Carey's shoulder. "You stole many years from us, separating us from our only son. We will never forget that. But we can see you've finally found a path worth walking, so we will choose to forgive you."

Carey bowed his head. "Thank you," he said, fighting back tears. His wife Bella passed him their son, whom he hoisted onto his hip, holding him close. "I couldn't imagine being apart from my child," he confessed.

"And I hope you never have to be," replied Henry's mother. She turned to her son. "Henry Fairchild, we have a lot of time to make up."

"Yes, we do," agreed the Dino Knight, pulling both his parents in for a hug.

EPILOGUE

Henry stroked his dinosaur's snout through the window of his bedroom.

"I'll be there in a minute, Rex."

The smell of breakfast lured Henry down the wooden stairs of the small cottage where he found his parents preparing the morning meal.

"You'll be late for training," remarked his father.

"He can't go anywhere until he's eaten up," said his mother with a smile.

For a moment, Henry felt as if he were in

a dream – but it was real. He felt at peace, finally reunited with his long-lost parents and living back in Brecklan.

Several weeks had passed since the Battle of the Dry Lands. Henry and his friends, both new and old, had won the day. But Henry had learnt an important lesson that would haunt him forever: no matter how much you want to live in peace, some people will try to take what you have, forcing a fight.

He finally understood why Lord Harding had established the Dino Knights, to guard against evil that lay in wait, always just out of sight.

With his parents back in his life, his friends by his side and his trusty T-Rex under his command, Henry was proud to protect Brecklan and help those in need. If called upon, he would be ready to fight for what was right. After breakfast.

THE END

Dinosaur-spotting in Panterra
A PRACTICAL FIELD GUIDE
by Henry Fairchild
Stable Boy, Dino Knight

There are many types of dinosaurs to be found in Brecklan, and even more roaming across Panterra.

Some of them have names almost as big as the animals themselves. And some of those names can be hard to say and even harder to spell. So, I've decided to create a field guide to the dinosaurs you are likely to see in Panterra, including help on how to pronounce their names.

Not all of the dinos here feature in this book, but you can read more about those who don't, and who uses them, in *Panterra in Peril* and *Invasion*.

Good luck dino-spotting!

Albertosaurus *(Al-bert-oh-sore-us)*
Smaller than the T-Rex, but no less fierce, the meat-eating Albertosaurus is Sir Neville Avingdon's preferred mount when he rides instead of flies.

Allosaurus *(Al-oh-sore-us)*
A large bipedal predator, similar to the T-Rex but smaller in size. Captain Carey's choice to ride into battle against the Guild.

Ankylosaur *(Ank-ee-lo-sore)*

The Ankylosaur is a low, solid animal covered in thick, spiky scales. The Ankylosaur has a deadly tail that can knock other dinosaurs sideways. Iyla's dinosaur is of this kind, and is called ***Conker***.

Brontosaurus *(Bron-tow-sore-us)*

A gentle giant with a long neck and very long tail. This massive herbivore is too big for Brecklan but has been rumoured to roam on the great plains of eastern Panterra.

Deinonychus *(Die-non-i-cuss)*
This dinosaur is one of the many types of raptor.

Dilophosaurus *(Dy-loff-oh-sore-us)*
This dinosaur has two ridges on its head and a fan that enlarges from its neck.

Hypsilophodon (*Hip-sill-oh-fo-don*)
This dinosaur walks on two legs and has scales. The Hypsilophodon is a herbivore and likes to eat Brecklan berries.

Nothronychus (*Noth-ron-ee-chus*)
Torin's dino, called **Haringey**, stands on two legs and has feathers that look a bit like fur from a distance.

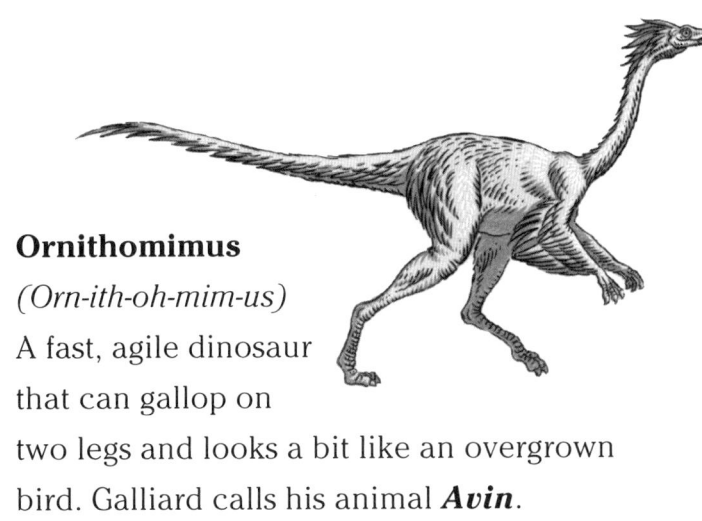

Ornithomimus
(Orn-ith-oh-mim-us)
A fast, agile dinosaur that can gallop on two legs and looks a bit like an overgrown bird. Galliard calls his animal ***Avin***.

Pachycephalosaurus
(Pack-ee-seff-al-oh-sore-us)
A bipedal dinosaur with a domed head that it uses for both offense and defence. Hannah selected this dinosaur to ride.

Parasaurolophus *(Pair-a-sore-ol-oh-fuss)*
This dinosaur has a hollow horn atop its head that is used for making sounds. These are Lord Harding's preferred animals for pulling his carriage because he likes the horn-sounds they make when they announce his arrival.

Pterosaur *(Tear-oh-sore)*
A winged creature, but not strictly a dinosaur. Sir Neville Avingdon was breeding an air force of these flying beasts.

Spinosaurus *(Spin-oh-sore-us)*
This fierce carnivore is Prince Pattick's dinosaur of choice, probably because he likes the impressive 'sail' on its back which is made up of vertical neural spines.

Stenonychosaurus *(Sten-oh-nick-oh-sore-uss)*
A small, feathered bipedal dinosaur with long legs. Hannah once tried to keep one as a pet until it ran off.

Styracosaurus *(Sty-rah-co-sore-us)*
This dino has six spikes on its head.
This is Ellie's dino,
called **Kayla**.

Triceratops *(Try-ser-a-tops)*
A lumbering herbivore (plant-eater) that has three horns on its head. My favourite Triceratops is called **Tribus**.

Tyrannosaurus Rex *(Tie-ran-oh-sore-us Rex)*
A large, fierce carnivore (meat-eater). T-Rexes are known to roam wild in Panterra, and nobody believed they could be tamed.

Utahraptor *(You-tah-rap-tor)*
This dinosaur is a raptor. Raptors are very intelligent and hunt in packs. They are the choice of the Royal Guardians of Volcanica.

Praise for
DINO KNIGHTS

PANTERRA IN PERIL

'*You like knights? You like dinosaurs? Watch out, your head might just explode. A simple but effective mash-up for newish readers and fans of* How to Train Your Dragon *and the* Beast Quest *series.*' THE TIMES

'*Combines a fun and imaginative story with some important messages of hope, courage, self-belief, and animal cruelty.*' BOOKS FOR TOPICS

'*I thoroughly enjoyed reading this book. It is fast-paced and packed full of action and adventure.*' READING ZONE

INVASION

'*With atmospheric illustrations, a gallery of amazing characters, a map, playful heraldic chapter headings and a dinosaur field guide, this exciting story of bravery, loyalty, friendship and family is perfect for all fearless young adventurers.*'
LANCASHIRE EVENING POST

'*Norton, loved for his stories which create compelling characters, awesome escapades and immersive worlds, is on his best form in this new tale.*' BOOKED

'*I think they might just be the best illustrations I have ever seen.*' TOPPSTA REVIEWER

'*Perfect for early or reluctant readers.*' BIG ISSUE NORTH

**Discover free games and resources at
www.scallywagpress.com/resources**